Valentine an

A Romantic Mel

As Performed at the Theatre-Royal Covent-Garden

Thomas Dibdin

Alpha Editions

This edition published in 2024

ISBN : 9789362095930

Design and Setting By
Alpha Editions
www.alphaedis.com
Email - info@alphaedis.com

As per information held with us this book is in Public Domain.
This book is a reproduction of an important historical work. Alpha Editions uses the best technology to reproduce historical work in the same manner it was first published to preserve its original nature. Any marks or number seen are left intentionally to preserve its true form.

Contents

CHARACTERS.	- 1 -
ACT I.	- 3 -
ACT II.	- 17 -

CHARACTERS.

FRENCH.

Pepin, *King of France*	Mr. CORY.
Henry, } *his Relations*	{ Mr. KLANERT.
Haufray, }	{ Mr. CLAREMONT.
Valentine, (*a Foundling*)	Mr. FARLEY.
Orson, (*a Wild Man*)	Mr. DUBOIS.
Hugo, (*Valentine's Armourer*)	Mr. BLANCHARD.
Blandiman, (*Page to the Empress*)	Mr. CHAPMAN.
Page to Valentine,	Master BLANCHARD.

Peers of France, Messrs. Curties, Lee, &c.

Citizens of Orleans, Messrs. Abbot, Atkins, Truman, &c.

Peasants and Pilgrims, Messrs. Byrne, Darley, King, Street, &c.

Choristers, Messrs. Kenrick, Linton, Odwell, Tett, Thomas, &c.

Alexander, *Emperor of Greece*,	Mr. FIELD.
Princess Eglantine,	Mrs. St. LEDGER.
Empress Belisanta, *Sister to the King*,	Mrs. DIBDIN.
Florimonda, *of Aquitaine*,	Mrs. FREDERICK.
Female Pilgrim,	Miss MARTYR.
Agatha, (*Attendant on Eglantine*)	Mrs. MARTYR.
Cicely, (*an old Peasant*)	Mrs. POWELL.

Nuns, Mesdames Atkins, Benson, Bologna, Burnet, Castelle, Gaudry, Iliff, Leserve, Price, Wheatley, &c.

SARACENS.

The Sorcerer Agramant (*the Green Knight*)	Mr. BOLOGNA, jun.
Iman,	Mr. HARLEY.
The Giant Ferragus,	Mons. LE GRAND.
The Genius Pacolet,	Master MENAGE.
Golden Oracle,	Mr. CRESSWELL.
Guardian of the Giant's Castle,	Mr. POWERS.

The other Characters by Messrs. L. Bologna, Lewiss, Platt, Sarjant, Wilde.—Mrs. Blurton, Mrs. Bologna, Miss Cox, Miss Dibdin, Mrs. Findlay, Mrs. Masters, Mrs. Norton, Mrs. Watts, Miss Willis, Mrs. Whitmore, &c.

The Scenery by RICHARDS PHILLIPS, WHITMORE, HOLLOGAN, &c.—The Decorations and Machinery by GOOSTREES, SLOPER, and CRESSWELL.

ACT I.

SCENE I.—*A long Perspective of the Suburbs of Orleans, terminating with the ancient City Gates— On one Side a Convent, the Windows of which are illuminated from within—The Stage is at first dark, which gives Effect to the Transparency of the Windows—As the Curtain rises slowly, the following choral Chaunt, accompanied by the Organ, is heard from the Interior of the Monastery.*

Hear, while our choral numbers flow,
Hear! and avert the awful doom,
Which human frailty fears below,
When summon'd to the insatiate tomb.

The Monastery Gates open, and the Friars and Nuns enter in Procession, singing the following

CHORUS.

Now bolder raise the hallow'd strain,
While living worth we haste to meet,
Our King, victorious comes again,
Again our foes sustain defeat.

They cross to the opposite Side, and exeunt while singing.——As they go off, the Stage becomes lighter (descriptive Music) The Dawn reddens, and the Sun rises over the City; the Gates of which are thrown open, HUGO, *with a Mob of Citizens, Soldiers, and Peasantry, come shouting down to the Front of the Stage, the Music ceases and* HUGO *speaks.*

HUGO.

Stop! stop! stop! now don't be in such a plaguy hurry. The holy brethren and sisters are just before us, and you, with your noise, would interrupt their merry solemnity.

First CITIZEN.

Merry solemnity, do you call it?

HUGO.

Ay, truly—they have just chaunted a solemn requiem in annual memory of the king's departed sister—and now, a merry occasion calls them forth to meet our good old king himself, who has been fighting for his people, conquered his foes, and deserves the thanks of all his friends.

Second CITIZEN.

Then why stand we here?

HUGO.

Why not? The king will pass through that gate, for the opening of which we have so long waited—and instead of going to the *show*, if we tarry a few moments, the *show* will come to us.

Third CITIZEN.

They say the king's favourite, young Valentine, hath gained great honour in these wars.

HUGO.

That he hath:—and humble though I seem, I have helped him to no small part of it.

All.

You!

HUGO.

To be sure—I made the very sword with which he slew the Saracens; and I defy any man to be killed with a better tempered weapon. Oh! I'll be bound he laid about him.—He had 'em here, and he had 'em there. (*Flourishing his stick to the annoyance of the mob.*)

Second CITIZEN.

But, friend Hugo, why shou'd the king lavish so much favour on a foundling?

Old WOMAN.

Aye, aye, he was found in a forest—Well, well, when great men go a-hunting, and find children in the woods, it's time for the fair sex to look about 'em.

Third CITIZEN.

And mark the end of it—In that very spot where Valentine was found, there has suddenly appeared a strange wild man, some say he is fourteen feet high.

Second CITIZEN.

No, no; thirteen feet and a half.

Third CITIZEN.

Who, to feed an old weather-beaten she-bear, bears down all before him.

First CITIZEN.

Nay, but Valentine is well-beloved among us too: the old men admire him, and his courtesy has gained him the hearts of all the young women.

Old WOMAN.

He never said a civil thing to me in all his life.

HUGO.

There it is—his honesty has made him enemies. There's Henry and Haufray, the cousins of the king, have determined to destroy him, because one is said to want to be heir to the throne, by marrying the king's daughter, the Princess Eglantine; and the other conceits himself to be the only man in the kingdom, fit for the office of captain general over all our victorious armies. Stand aside!—Here come all our noble peers to meet the king.

GRAND MARCH.

The Peers of France advance from the Gate to meet the king, who enters with the following

ORDER OF PROCESSION.

An Officer.

Banner of France.

Men at Arms, two and two.

Officer.

Banner.

Soldiers with Spears and Shields.

Choristers, two and two.

Grand Cross.

Lady Abbess.

Choristers.

Grand Crozier.

Nuns and Friars, two and two.

Black Musicians.

Officer bearing the Oriflamme.

Peers of France, two and two.

The King.

Pages and Armour bearers.

Henry and Haufray.

Officer.

Red Banner.

Men at Arms.

Officer.

Banner.

Soldiers.

Page with Valentine's Standard.

Valentine.

Saracen General and Officers in Chains.

The Chorus forms an Accompaniment to the March.

CHORUS.

With the gladsome notes of victory,
Let the merry cymbals ring,
Till earth resounds a people's cry,
Whose hearts proclaim—
Long live the King!

During the Chorus the Characters are so arranged that the King is in the centre, and when the Music stops, he speaks:

KING.

This genuine welcome from my people is the most brilliant trophy I have gained:—but thank not *me*, my friends—to this young warrior's arm we owe success. (*pointing to Valentine*) The giant chieftain of yon pagan host measures his length on earth, subdued by valour and by Valentine.

VALENTINE.

My gracious liege; the child of chance, the creature of your bounty can never atchieve a thousandth part of what he owes to you, his sovereign, and his *father*.

KING.

Yet, in requital of that sense of honour, take from thy king the Earldom of Auvergne.

HENRY.

(*Apart to the King.*) Auvergne! a royal title!—He'll next obtain the crown—Sure, my liege, a man unknown—

KING.

It is my best prerogative to rescue unknown merit from obscurity.

HAUFRAY.

(*Aside.*) If this goes on, he will aspire to gain the princess. (*apart to the king*) Men of birth, great sir—

KING.

Will be most proud of him, whose zeal, at once, supports my crown, their honours, and the people's cause.

OFFICER.

Dread sir, your daughter, beauteous Eglantine, impatient waits you at the royal palace.

KING.

Tell her, we long to clasp her to a father's bosom. Captives, your lives were spared on the condition that you receive our faith (*the Saracens bow*). Be preparation made, and let Religion's triumph grace our feast. Auvergne, my daughter's lips, again, shall speak her father's thanks—Our citizens of Orleans ope' their gates with loyal welcome to receive their sovereign. Thus ever may the king and people of this happy land, endeared by firm affection to each other, own the dear ties of father and of children! and, woe to those, who, with a traitor's hand, would tear the bond asunder!—Lead on.

Exeunt in procession. The King and Attendants go off thro' the city gates—The Captives, accompanied by the Friars and Nuns, enter the Monastery.

SCENE II.—*Interior of the Convent.*

Enter BLANDIMAN *and* BELISANTA.

BELISANTA.

Have all retired? Are we observed, my friend?

BLANDIMAN.

The fathers seek their cells to offer prayers for the new converts.

BELISANTA.

Alas! 'tis now the twentieth year since I have sought the mournful consolation of recounting how much a wretched woman owes thy friendship.

BLANDIMAN.

Away with sorrow, and in this moment of rejoicing, demand an audience of the king, your brother.

BELISANTA.

He thinks his sister guilty. Was I not banished by my husband the Emperor of Greece, fatally wrought on by traiterous slander, when, you, alone, accompanied a weak, defenceless woman?

BLANDIMAN.

Never shall I forget when, wearied with anguish and fatigue, you sat beneath a blasted oak; the wind with mournful sound scattered the falling leaves—meanwhile your groans were echoed by the distant murmur of nightly prowling wolves.

BELISANTA.

When, at my request you left me, in the hope of finding human aid, two babes, the offspring of my unkind husband, first saw the light. Starting with agony, these eyes beheld one of my children in the savage gripe of a most hideous bear. One desperate effort, short as furious, impelled me to attempt pursuit. I fell, and knew no more of sense, till from a peasant's wife I learned that she had found and borne me to her humble dwelling.

BLANDIMAN.

I wandered far, till the sound of horns led me to where I met the king, who with a frown at hearing of your name, on pain of death, warned me to leave his presence.

BELISANTA.

Vainly I sought my infant left behind—reason a second time forsook her seat.—The sisters of this convent poured balm into my bosom, and religion, cloathed in the garb of patience, brought me peace.

BLANDIMAN.

Have you ne'er yet disclosed your name and rank?

BELISANTA.

Accounted dead, and masses for my soul's health yearly ordered, I vowed that as my children were for ever lost to me, my husband and my brother unconvinced of the cruel treacheries employed against me, ne'er to be known but as a sister of this order.

BLANDIMAN.

Yet may you hope that providence will watch o'er piety and innocence, and but to-day, I learned that Valentine, a favourite of the king's was found—

Enter a Friar.

FRIAR.

The duties of our order require your presence to join the Pagan captives in preparation for the sacred change they are about to make.

BELISANTA.

We attend you, father.——(*To* BLANDIMAN) The ceremony past, I wait your leisure—and for your friendly deeds, they'll meet reward from where I hope my prayers have long since registered them.

[*Exeunt.*

SCENE III.—*The Palace.*

(*Descriptive Music.*)

The KING *discovered on his Throne, attended by* VALENTINE, HENRY, HAUFRAY, *and the Peers of France—the Princess is announced by her Ladies, and enters—the* KING *presents* VALENTINE *to her as the Preserver of his Life, she receives him with a warmth of Gratitude approaching to Love—the* KING *leads her to a Seat, resumes his Throne, and speaks:*

KING.

Be it proclaimed that any of my subjects who have petitions to our throne, may now approach. The best acknowledgement we offer heaven for good received, is when we use the ample power it gives to bless our people.—The greatest monarch he, whose subjects are the happiest.——Let all enter.

The Music plays a characteristic Symphony—a Group of Peasantry enter, the Principal of whom unfolds a Petition, and while he and the rest kneel, recites the following

CHAUNT.

With lowly respect, zeal, devotion, and duty,
To your Majesty's state, and our Princess's beauty,
We entreat that you'll graciously grant us assistance
Against a wild man, who in spite of resistance,
Whoe'er in his road he may meet with, destroys,
And your peaceable subjects and liegemen annoys,
Then let your brave knights take this wild-man away,
And your humble petitioners shall ever pray.
Chorus—Then let, &c.

KING.

What armed force will undertake this enterprize? When a savage strikes at the general safety, 'tis the duty of all good citizens to join against him.

HENRY.

Haply, young Valentine, in gratitude for the high favours he receives, would gladly go alone on such an errand.

HAUFRAY.

Ay, good my liege, his all-subduing valour must succeed.

VALENTINE.

For once, whate'er your motives you're my friends. It had been arrogance, had *I*, before so many gallant knights, proposed myself; but now I swear, living or dead, to bring this fell destroyer to your presence, or in the forest he inhabits, leave this form a worthless token of his victory.

(Pantomime Music.)

VALENTINE *takes a respectful Leave of the* KING, *and an affectionate one of* EGLANTINE, *who seems to reproach* HENRY *and* HAUFRAY *with causing his departure*—VALENTINE *goes off with the Peasants; the* KING, *&c. on the opposite Side——The Scene closes.*

SCENE IV.—*An Apartment in the Palace.*

Enter HUGO, *furbishing* VALENTINE's *Shield.*

There—I have made Lord Valentine's shield so bright, that if the wild man does but see his face in it, he may haply take fright at his own ugly features. It's monstrous unlucky that though I have been armour-bearer and armour-maker to the young knight from the time of his first campaign, yet something has always happened to prevent my going with him, and now when so handsome an opportunity offers, I'm sadly afraid I shan't be able to find an excuse for staying behind. I've been ill of every thing I could think of, in turn, and have obtained more certificates of bad health, than would have paid for the cure of real sickness.—Let's see—what can I think of next?

Enter AGATHA.

AGATHA.

So, Mr. Hugo, your poor master is going again, I fear?

HUGO.

Yes, I fear we are both going. But you see how it is with us—a willing horse, you know——

AGATHA.

The poor princess will cry her eyes out, she's so sorry——

HUGO.

And so am I.

AGATHA.

You sorry!—for what?

HUGO.

Why, to think that——that——

AGATHA.

Oh, I know what you are sorry for—you've heard that Valentine has sworn to go alone, and that you will lose the honour of sharing in so hopeful an enterprize.

HUGO.

Has he? how lucky! (*aside*) Yes, I'm monstrous sorry—I didn't know it sooner. (*apart*)

AGATHA.

I knew you'd feel hurt.

HUGO.

True—to think I that carried him in arms, when a boy, should see him go *alone* at these years.

AGATHA.

Well, but if you were to ask him.———

HUGO.

What, to break his vow? I wou'dn't have such a sin at my door, for the honour of fighting the wildest man in Christendom.

Enter VALENTINE, *with a Letter.*

VALENTINE.

Agatha, present this to the princess, and tell her till Valentine can prove that gentle blood flows in his veins, her roseate cheek shall ne'er have cause to blush for him she has so honoured.

AGATHA. (*gives* VALENTINE *a Scarf.*)

Sir, she sends this parting token, and will pray incessantly for your return.

[*Exit.*

VALENTINE.

Then success is certain! Come, see my armour.

HUGO.

(*While arming him.*) I humbly hope, my lord, that, now, I have no hinderance you'll graciously permit my services. I have kill'd divers wild things in my time, and might be useful.

VALENTINE.

Well, then, thou shalt go with me.

HUGO.

(*Dropping the armour.*) Shall I! O dear!

VALENTINE.

How now?

HUGO.

'Twas but a sudden qualm—That was a real pain i' the back.

[*Aside.*

VALENTINE.

I mean to take thee but to the entrance of the forest.

HUGO.

I cou'dn't think of intruding further.

VALENTINE.

There secure my horse, and wait my return. (*Draws his sword.*) Now gentle fortune aid thy knight.

And let the Fates for good or ill combine,
The star that leads me on, is, Eglantine.

[*Exeunt on opposite sides.*

SCENE V.—*The Forest of Orleans.* (Richards.)

On one side a large Tree which can be climbed, at the back, a Cavern nearly covered with Underwood.

The Peasants *enter who presented the Petition at Court.*

First PEASANT.

Well, the king hath heard our petition, and here we go joyfully on our way home.

Second PEASANT.

Troth, I am weary;—let us rest awhile; for when the wild man is once killed, this forest will be quite safe, and things will run in the right road again.

Third PEASANT.

For my part I fear nothing but the wild man—Lack-a-day! it would do you good only, an't were to hear him roar—

(*Music heard without.*)

Mercy on us? What was that?

First PEASANT.

That was no honest roaring. Such sweet sounds mean no good. I have rested enough now.

[*Going.*

Second Peasant.

Don't hurry so, goodman Ambrose, the music is not so bad.

Third Peasant.

No matter—I wou'dn't dance with old nick for a partner, to the prettiest tune that ever was composed.

[*Exeunt.*

Enter Three Pilgrims, *who join in the following*

GLEE.

(*Accompanied by one of them on the lute.*)

"*Pilgrims.* The sun to ocean hies away.
"The curfeu bell is ringing,"
And pilgrims thro' the twilight grey,
"Now cheer the way by singing.
"While each, tho' weary, feels delight,
"In thinking of his inn at night,
"And ev'ry footstep moves in time,
"As plays the distant village chime."

Re-enter the Peasants running.

Peasants. Mercy on us!

Pilgrims.
Strangers, say—

Peasants. Here he comes,

Pilgrims.
Which is our way?

Peasants. Have you seen him?

Pilgrims.
Whom?

Peasants.
He's coming.
Hark! the wild man—

Pilgrims.
Tell us, pray.

Peasants. Here you must not stand humdrumming.
Yes, 'tis he—away! away!

All.
Away! away!

[*Exeunt hastily.*

Characteristic Music, which varies with the Incidents of the following Scene.

A strange kind of howling is heard—ORSON *presents himself with an animal in his grasp, which he has just slain—a faint roar is heard of the old Bear—*ORSON *expresses satisfaction, intimating he has got food for her. The Bear enters—*ORSON *shews her the food, and in a playful manner, follows her into the cave.*

VALENTINE *enters, followed at cautious distance by* HUGO, *who puts down a basket containing some cordage, fruits, and a flask, and seems very anxious to be dismissed—* VALENTINE, *in dumb shew, charges him with a token for* EGLANTINE *and the* KING, *and recommending himself to heaven, takes his way into the thicket.*

HUGO, *being left alone, seems terrified, and as much afraid to go back, as to follow* VALENTINE—*looks warily about him, hears a noise, and runs to the cave for shelter— a roar is heard from the cave,* HUGO *instantly returns running, most whimsically terrified, and pursued by* ORSON—HUGO *throws his cloak at the wild man, and while he is tearing it to pieces,* HUGO *runs off—*ORSON *throws down the cloak, and doubly enraged by the escape of his intended victim, follows.*

VALENTINE *re-enters, cannot find the wild man—sees* HUGO'*s cloak, laments his supposed death, and mounts a tree to look out for his enemy.*

ORSON *re-enters, and expresses disappointment at not having overtaken* HUGO—*as he approaches the tree where* VALENTINE *is,* VALENTINE *plucks a branch, and throws it at him—*ORSON *looks up with astonishment, chatters uncouthly to* VALENTINE, *throws the branch back to him, and beckons him to come down—*VALENTINE *hesitates—*ORSON *enraged, immediately ascends the tree—and while he is climbing up one side,* VALENTINE *gets down on the other, and in turn beckons his opponent.—* ORSON *makes but one jump from the tree to the ground—runs to* VALENTINE, *who opposes his polished shield—*ORSON *seeing his own figure reflected in it, suddenly starts back—*VALENTINE, *with his sword drawn, keeps* ORSON *at bay, and leads him round the stage, still wondering at the figure he sees.—*ORSON *at length struggles for the shield, takes it from* VALENTINE, *and throws it away—*VALENTINE *has another shield at his back, which he immediately uses, slightly wounds* ORSON *with the point of his sword,* *at which he, enraged, looks round for a weapon, pulls up a young tree by the roots, and uses it as a club.*

A fierce combat ensues—VALENTINE, *by his lightness and activity, escapes many dreadful blows, aimed at him by* ORSON.—*They stand to breathe awhile, when the Bear suddenly totters from the cave*—VALENTINE, *at the moment she opens her mouth, presents his sword in the attitude of thrusting it down her throat*—ORSON, *as if instinctively apprised of the danger of his foster-mother, drops his club, and seems to implore mercy for the old and feeble Bear*—VALENTINE *retires, the Bear follows*—ORSON *recovers his club, and is about to attack* VALENTINE, *when the latter cuts* ORSON'*s hand—the club falls, and* VALENTINE *is once more attacking the Bear, when* ORSON *supplicates*—VALENTINE *suddenly throws a cord round* ORSON'*s hands, and bids him follow him*—VALENTINE *holding the other end of the cord.*—ORSON *looks at the Bear, and then at* VALENTINE, *who throws him fruit—he gives it to the Bear*—VALENTINE *gives him wine from a flask, he tastes it, likes it, and gives some to the Bear, who seems half strangled with it, and totters towards the cave.*

VALENTINE *again bids* ORSON *follow him*—ORSON *suddenly snaps the cord, and follows the Bear—the Bear unable to reach the cave, drops with a faint roar, and dies, as if from old age.*

ORSON *shakes her, puts the food and bottle by her, throws himself on the ground, and seems to weep.*

VALENTINE *ventures to caress him*—ORSON *turns short on him, snatches at his sword by the blade, and again cuts his fingers—resumes his club, but throws it down again on seeing the dead Bear.*—VALENTINE *caresses* ORSON *again (still keeping on his guard),* ORSON *seeing* VALENTINE'*s attention to himself and the Bear, seems pleased and overcome by it—presents* VALENTINE *with one end of the cord, and holding the other, suffers himself to be led off, looking back from time to time, at the dead Bear, and making an uncouth and mournful kind of lamentation.*

ACT II.

SCENE I.—*A Court-Yard of the Palace at Orleans*—(Phillips.)— *in front a pair of great Gates, with Posts before them, and a Chain across from one to the other.*

(Pantomime Music.)

Officers and Servants run on terrified—go in at the great gates, and make them fast— VALENTINE *enters on horseback, leading* ORSON, *who seems amazed at every thing around him—* VALENTINE *blows a horn at the gate,* ORSON *is surprised at the noise, tries to blow it, but cannot, which makes him very angry—Some one looks out from above, sees* ORSON, *shakes his head and retires—* ORSON *imitates him—* VALENTINE *angrily tries to force the gate, but is unable;* ORSON *assists, without effect—at length, seeing that* VALENTINE *is eager to obtain entrance,* ORSON *pulls up a post, breaks the chain by which it is attached to the next post, and batters the gate open—attendants rush out armed, are going to attack* ORSON—VALENTINE *interposes—* HENRY *and* HAUFRAY *enter, shake hands with* VALENTINE—HENRY, *in turning from* VALENTINE, *half draws his sword,* ORSON *sees him, and pushes it rudely back into the scabbard—* VALENTINE *signifies to* ORSON *that he must shake hands with his friends—he takes a hand of each, and squeezes them violently—he then shakes hands with the others—* EGLANTINE *enters, runs into* VALENTINE's *arms—* ORSON *is astonished, delighted at her beauty, he runs to embrace her, as* VALENTINE *has done, but is repulsed and much displeased at it—* VALENTINE *makes him kneel and kiss her hand—drums and trumpets are heard, the wild man is alarmed—the* KING *and Courtiers enter and welcome* VALENTINE—ORSON's *attention is still fixed on the Princess—he approaches her again, she, terrified, runs for protection to* VALENTINE—ORSON *seems hurt, and makes a savage kind of moaning—the* KING *admires* ORSON, *who wants to shake hands with him, but is taught the proper mode of approaching him by* VALENTINE—*the* KING *orders* ORSON *a dress, and goes off with the Princess and attendants—* VALENTINE *and* ORSON *are following, when the latter espies* HUGO, *and remembering the adventure of the cloak in the forest, runs furiously towards him, and reminds him of it by action—* VALENTINE *interposes in behalf of his terrified armour-bearer, whom he reconciles to* ORSON, *and leaves them together—Attendants bring on apparel, as ordered by the* KING, *for* ORSON, *who makes many whimsical mistakes in putting it on, when suddenly missing* VALENTINE, *he throws the dress at the Officers, and runs into the palace in search of his friend.*

SCENE II.—*An Apartment in the Palace.* (Phillips.)

(Laughing heard without.)

Re-Enter HUGO.

HUGO.

Ha! ha! ha! the wild man has began to shew his breeding with a vengeance—he has overturned the kitchen, set the cellar afloat, and sent every thing in the stable to rack and manger; for he hath eaten the beast's provender, given wine to the horses, and thrown the cook into the dripping pan, where he basted him with his own ladle.

Enter AGATHA.

AGATHA.

Ah, Hugo—what, are you laughing at the wild man? I'm sure he frightens me.

HUGO.

He'd have frightened you more, if you had seen him, as I did, in his own dining room in the forest.

AGATHA.

Why now, really, had you courage enough to venture there?

HUGO.

To be sure I had—I went in boldly—by mistake.

(*Aside.*)

AGATHA.

When he was out, I suppose?

HUGO.

O, no; he was there, and wanted me to stay. I took off my cloak to oblige him, and to avoid ceremony, came away without it. Your lady may well be glad that Valentine had power to tame him.

AGATHA.

Glad! she's more uneasy than ever; and if she hasn't fallen *out* of *love* into *jealousy*, I'll give you leave to say that Agatha is no conjuror.

HUGO.

I'm sure I never said you was one: but who is she jealous of?

AGATHA.

You shall hear. The Duke of Acquitane has arrived to beg relief against a pagan, they call the Green Knight, who holds his daughter unlawfully a prisoner, and unless, by a certain hour she is rescued, she will be forced to marry this Saracen monster, who has already vanquished and hanged up twenty knights who fought for her.

HUGO.

Poor fellows! And what is he to have who conquers the pagan?

AGATHA.

The lady's hand.

HUGO.

Hanging on one side, and marriage on the other! bless me! Where could they find twenty knights mad enough to undertake such a terrible alternative?

AGATHA.

Why; your master, Valentine, will go, if it's only for the honour of the thing: and the Princess is distracted lest he should fall in love with the lady, or be killed by the knight.

HUGO.

And for fear he shou'd once more ask me to bear him company I'll get out of the way as fast as possible.

(*Going, meets the* PRINCESS.)

EGLANTINE.

Hugo, where are you going?

HUGO.

I'm going, madam, to——to unarm my master before the banquet, and fear I shall be too late.

EGLANTINE.

Hold, sir—Can you be secret?

HUGO.

Ask Agatha, your grace's hand-maid—she knows I can.

AGATHA.

I know you are a blockhead. Mark my lady.

EGLANTINE.

Can you not bring, Sir Valentine's armour to Agatha's apartment?

HUGO.

Aye, madam, if she be there to receive it—but when, and how long must I—

AGATHA.

How rude of you to want to know more than I do—Go, fetch the armour, quick!

EGLANTINE.

And here's a purse of gold to speed thee.

HUGO.

I lack no spur but your commands, and a kiss from Agatha.

AGATHA.

No, no—(*he is going away*) Well, take it.

HUGO.

Now, why did you say no, no?

AGATHA.

Why, one must refuse at first for decency.

EGLANTINE.

Here, Hugo.

[*Gives the purse.*

HUGO.

[*Takes it.*] Madam, I'm gone.

AGATHA.

[*Apart to* HUGO.] I thought you didn't want the money.

HUGO.

One must refuse at first, you know, for decency.

[*Exit.*

EGLANTINE.

In Valentine's disguise I'll see this beauty he would venture for;—for, should he conquer in the fight, how many Cupids smiling, through her tears, may aim at Valentine! And, shou'd he fall——

AGATHA.

It wou'd be a sad thing, truly, my dear lady; but how will your going help it?

EGLANTINE.

There is a prophecy, that no *man nursed by woman* can subdue this pagan—Perhaps it is his fate to fall by woman.

AGATHA.

He wou'dn't be the first if he did, madam.

EGLANTINE.

My mother's martial spirit trained me up to Amazonian sports—Foremost in the chace, thrice have I pierced the monarch of our woods; and, more than once, have been where battles roar, and undismayed, beheld the mortal conflict.

AGATHA.

I shou'd have been frighten'd out of my wits.

EGLANTINE.

By force or stratagem it may be mine to free this lady, and save my lover from a double danger.

AGATHA.

But will he go, knowing this prophecy?

EGLANTINE.

He disregards it as an artful fable, coined by the Saracen; or else as pagan sorcery, which he, a christian knight, fears not to combat with. Come, thou, as my page, shalt follow me, and learn my purpose on the journey.

AGATHA.

Me!

Enter HUGO.

HUGO.

The armour is all in Agatha's apartment, your highness. My master had taken it all off before I came.

AGATHA.

But, madam, wont you go to the banquet, you purposely provided for the king and Valentine?

EGLANTINE.

No time for feasting now—obey my orders——We'll to the Green Knight's Camp——Away, my girl.

[*Exit.*

"AGATHA.

"With all my heart. Its my opinion my lady is so in love, that, to save Valentine from danger, she'd follow him to the world's end.

"HUGO.

"I dare say she would, but when I am in danger nobody talks of following me.

"AGATHA.

"No; that's impossible—you run so fast.

DUET.—HUGO and AGATHA.

"*Hugo.*
The man who fights and runs away,
"*Agatha.*
Wou'd make a sorry lover,
"*Hugo.*
May live to fight another day,
"*Agatha.*
But ne'er his fame recover.
"While he who boldly meets the foe,
"*Hugo.*
May boldly die, 'tis true,
"*Agatha.*
Will live in history, you know,
"*Hugo.*
I'd rather live with you.
"Nay come I'll boldly meet the foe,
"*Agatha.* I'll love you if you do;
"*Hugo.*
And when to fame I'm wed you know,

"*Agatha.*
Then I'll be wed to you.
"*Both.*
Then I'll be wed to you.

II.

"*Agatha.* The hero slain, claims beauty's tear,
"*Hugo.*
Her smiles more pleasure giving;
"*Agatha.*
She holds his mem'ry ever dear,
"*Hugo.*
And marries some one living.
"But come, I'll bravely meet the foe, &c.

"[*Exeunt.*"

SCENE III.—*A grand Banquet under Pavilions in the Palace Gardens.* (Hollogan.)

The KING; *and* VALENTINE *(unarmed) discovered in great state, Nobles and Ladies seated at the Banquet Tables, &c.*

ORSON *enters, pleased at the sight, goes from one table to the other—the* KING *orders him wine, he imitates their manner of drinking—takes another cup, is going to drink,* VALENTINE *tells him to be careful, pointing to his head, indicating that wine will intoxicate him,* ORSON *does not understand him—a Servant entering with wine, he forces it from him, and goes off with it—the Princess's Ladies enter, much alarmed at missing her, and bring with them her cloathes.*

VALENTINE *calls for* HUGO, *who informs him that the Princess bribed him to let her have* VALENTINE*'s armour to go to the Green Knight's camp—*VALENTINE, *goes off, followed by the* KING, *&c. in search of* EGLANTINE.—ORSON *re-enters, and from the effects of the wine, appears half intoxicated—*HUGO *sits down at the table, pours out a goblet of wine, when* ORSON *suddenly takes it out of his hand, shewing him, by pointing to his head, in* VALENTINE*'s manner, it is not good for him; he misses* VALENTINE, *runs anxiously about, seems to enquire of* HUGO, *looks under the tables, and in every place, and at last tears his hair, stamps, and throws himself on the ground—*HUGO, *alarmed, runs off.—*ORSON *rises, once more looks about for* VALENTINE, *and not seeing him, goes distractedly off, leaping over the tables, and overturning all before him.*

SCENE IV.—*A Wood.* (Richards.)

Enter AGATHA, *dressed as a* Page.

AGATHA.

There goes my lady, drest and arm'd so like Sir Valentine, that if he were to meet her, he'd think it were a second self. She bade me follow at some distance to avoid suspicion, and mislead any who might pursue her—I fear she will prove but a weak defender of the poor Lady Florimonda, who, if Sir Valentine do not quickly overtake us, must, of force, be married to the pagan sorcerer.

ROMANCE.

'Tis far away o'er yonder plains,
A cruel pagan tyrant reigns,
And holds a christian maid in chains,
Ah, well-a-day, poor lady!

II.

And ev'ry day some gallant knight,
Who strives to win this lady's right,
Is by the pagan slain in fight.
Ah, well-a-day, poor lady!

III.

And ere the sun forsake the sky,
Unless more powerful aid is nigh,
The pagan she must *wed,* or *die.*
Ah, well-a-day, poor lady!

IV.

And, now, fair Eglantine is gone,
By jealous pangs her bosom torn,
To save her love, or die forlorn.
Ah, well-a-day, poor lady!

[*Exit.*

Enter HENRY *and* HAUFRAY, *from opposite sides.*

HENRY.

This way, my friend, our foe is in our power. Yonder he walks in *armour,* but *alone.*

HAUFRAY.

Nay, Henry, this way lies the road—Unarm'd he comes perhaps to meet the princess.

HENRY.

Your jealousy has blinded you. I say with swiftest pace he there eludes our vengeance, close followed by his page.

HAUFRAY.

Ambition makes you mad. Stand back, and as he passes, unprotected by his wild associate, here let's attack him.

HENRY.

You fear to face him. I'll believe my eyes and go alone. By heav'n, 'tis he indeed.

HAUFRAY.

Now will you believe your eyes?

*They conceal themselves—*VALENTINE *enters, and is attacked by* HAUFRAY, *who is overthrown, when* HENRY *aims a blow behind* VALENTINE—ORSON *suddenly enters, catches* HENRY *up, and carries him away—*HAUFRAY *is beaten off by* VALENTINE, *who follows—*ORSON *re-enters, signifies that he has thrown* HENRY *into the river, but not finding* VALENTINE *where he left him, the wild man picks up the swords of the disarmed adversaries, and runs off, in pursuit of him.*

SCENE V.—*The Encampment and Pavilion of the Green Knight.—on one Side a large Oak Tree, on which several Knights in shining Armour, are seen hanging—on the other Side is a Tree, to which a Shield, marked with magical Characters, is suspended, and guarded by a Saracen Priest.* (Phillips.)

The Lady FLORIMONDA *discovered embroidering a Scarf—She hears a distant march, looks out in hopes of some Knight's approach—the Green Knight enters, in brilliant armour, preceded by Saracen Warriors—he offers the Lady* FLORIMONDA *his hand, which she rejects, and shews him these words, embroidered on the scarf:*

"Florimonda will wed the Knight,
who frees her from Agramant."

He threatens, and strikes the scarf from her hand—she falls on her knees in despair—a trumpet is sounded without—AGRAMANT *orders it to be answered*—EGLANTINE *enters, and offers to fight with him—the Green Knight points to the tree where the other knights are hanging, and disdaining the youthful appearance of* EGLANTINE, *advises her to avoid the combat—she insists on a trial—they fight—she is overthrown—the Green Knight is about to put her to death, when* VALENTINE *rushes on, discovers* EGLANTINE, *and fiercely defies* AGRAMANT, *who, in derision, bids him try to pull down the shield from the tree—when* VALENTINE *approaches the shield, the Saracen Priest interposes, and speaks:*

PRIEST.

Forbear!—this shield protects a prince not nursed by woman.

VALENTINE *persists, and encounters the Green Knight, with battle-axe, broad sword, &c.*—VALENTINE *is worsted*—ORSON *rushes on, and begs to fight* AGRAMANT—VALENTINE *recollects the words of the priest, and bids* ORSON *try to pull away the shield—which he is about to seize, when the priest again says:*

Forbear!—this shield protects a prince not nursed by woman.

ORSON, *not regarding him, approaches the shield, and it flies into his hand—the Green Knight, forewarned of his fate, rushes on* ORSON *in savage desperation—but every weapon breaks on the enchanted shield*—ORSON *strikes* AGRAMANT *to the ground*—VALENTINE's *soldiers rush on, and vanquish the Saracens—thunder is heard, and the Genius* PACOLET *is seen descending on a flying horse—he alights, comes forward, and addresses the characters.*

PACOLET.

(*To Agram.*) Thine ill-earned laurels must to virtue yield,
(*To Orson*) While thou hast freed the Genius of the Shield;
To yonder castle haste (*To Valen.*) a golden head,
The wild-man's birth, and your's, shall truly read.
Then hence, brave knight, while honour you pursue,
This ring has power enchantment to subdue.

PACOLET *gives a ring to* VALENTINE, *waves his wand, they follow him.*

SCENE VI.—*Castle of the Giant Ferragus.* (Richards.)

VALENTINE *and* ORSON *enter, and approach the gates.* ORSON *seeing a horn, blows it—it utters a dreadfully discordant blast—the gates fly open—two Fiends rush out, one of them speaks.*

FIEND.

The invincible sovereign of this castle, the mighty and gigantic Ferragus, warns you to fly—hence!—begone!

They rush on VALENTINE *and* ORSON, *are overthrown and sink—as* VALENTINE *and* ORSON *are proceeding, a Lion enters,* VALENTINE *presents the magic ring, and the Lion disappears—*PACOLET *is seen in place of the monster, and conducts* VALENTINE *and* ORSON *into the Giant's dwelling.*

SCENE VII.—*A Magic Chamber in the Castle*—(Whitmore.)

In the Centre, on a Pillar, a golden Head, and on one side of it, stands the enormous Giant FERRAGUS, *leaning on a massive Club—*VALENTINE *and* ORSON *enter—the Giant raises his monstrous club—*PACOLET *enters—waves his wand, the club changes to a heavy chain, incircling the arms of the giant—*ORSON *catches up the giant, throws him down, and stands over him,* PACOLET *waves his wand.*

EGLANTINE, FLORIMONDA, *and* BELISANTA *enter.*

PACOLET *touches the Golden Oracle, which speaks as follows:*

ORACLE.

Hear!

ORSON *is alarmed—*PACOLET *makes a sign for silence, again touches the head, which proceeds to say:*

ORACLE.

Orson is endowed with reason!

ORSON *falls on his knees, and shews his sensibility by thanking the Gods—the head proceeds:*

GOLDEN ORACLE.

Valentine and Orson are brothers, and sons of the Emperor of Greece, and the much-wronged Empress Belisanta.

The Empress BELISANTA *throws off her Nun's dress, and appears as herself, embraces her sons, who embrace each other—*PACOLET *addresses the Oracle.*

PACOLET.

Agent of sorcery, thy task is o'er,[*the head falls, and the giant sinks.*
And thy gigantic master sinks, to rise no more.

ORSON *approaches* FLORIMONDA, *she still rejects him, he looks at his uncouth figure and dress, and rushes out, followed by* PACOLET, *but immediately returns, splendidly dressed—he again presses his suit to* FLORIMONDA, *she is pleased with him—the Empress joins the hands of* VALENTINE *and* ORSON *with* EGLANTINE *and* FLORIMONDA*—the Genius signifies his approbation, and thus addresses* BELISANTA.

PACOLET.

Lady, most wrong'd, rejoice!—your royal lord,
Repentant, comes with splendid honours due,
To suffering virtue, to a throne restored,
Days of delight remain for these and you.
While my task over, gaily hence I hie,
Distress still aiding, as I onward fly.
To realms of light and fields of liberty.

PACOLET *changes the scene, mounts his winged horse, and flies up, while the transformation is making from the Mystic Chamber to the last scene.*

SCENE VIII.—*A most brilliant Hall, hung round with all the ornamental Trophies and Devices of ancient Chivalry, disposed in long and varied perspective.*——
(Whitmore.)

The Emperor, &c. enter in

GRAND PROCESSION.

Soldiers of King Pepin's Guard.

Officers bearing Banners.

Choristers.

Captives, with Presents.

Guards.

Captives, with Presents.

A SUPERB PYRAMID,

containing

A MILITARY BAND.

Guards.

Valentine's Banner.

FIRST GRAND TROPHY,

on which are borne

VALENTINE AND EGLANTINE.

Guards.

SECOND GRAND TROPHY,

on which are borne

ORSON AND FLORIMONDA.

The Peers of France.

Attendants of the Emperor.

The Royal Banners of

France and Constantinople.

Dancers.

Ladies of the Court.

The Empress BELISANTA,

supported by

The EMPEROR,

and

The KING OF FRANCE.

The Characters come to the front of the stage, and the Piece concludes with the following

FINALE.

Moment of triumph! virtue's power,
Resplendent rising, gilds the day,
Surmounts misfortune's clouded hour,
And drives each wint'ry storm away.
Thrice, happy day!
Huzza! huzza!

FINIS.

Milton Keynes UK
Ingram Content Group UK Ltd.
UKHW040312181024
449757UK00005B/508